THE REST
MANAGERS'
& WAITER'S
—— GUIDE BOOK ——

HOW TO BE A GREAT SERVER, HANDLE DIFFICULT CUSTOMERS, EARN BIG TIPS & KEEP YOUR SANITY!

JAMES **CALDWELL** PATRICK **CALDWELL** MICHAEL **RATHKE**

The Restaurant Managers' and Waiters' Guide Book
How to be a Great Server, Handle Difficult Customers, Earn
Big Tips & Keep Your Sanity!

James Caldwell, Patrick Caldwell, Michael Rathke

Published by: Orange Brothers, Inc.
E-mail: info@getbiggertips.com

ISBN: 978-0692848616

BONUS FOR READERS OF THIS BOOK

Get a free copy of our "Rules for Restaurant Customers" which are 10 guidelines for the way we hope all customers could behave in restaurants.

Download your copy here: (www.GetBiggerTips.com)

TABLE OF CONTENTS

Introduction

Ten Steps to Becoming a Top Server

The Seven Most Annoying Customer Personalities & How to Handle Them

Afterword

About the Authors

INTRODUCTION

If we had it our way, everyone would be required to wait tables for a year as soon as they turned eighteen years old. Not only is serving others in an apron a humbling and grounding experience, but it also equips one with critical life skills: dealing with difficult people, collaborating, multitasking, working hard, and being selfless.

Interestingly, there is something transformational about restaurants that sometimes turns otherwise ordinary customers into impolite and rude characters. However, this phenomenon isn't limited to the patrons; restaurants also seem to lull some servers into the silly belief that certain behaviors that would never be accepted in any other workplace environment are somehow acceptable in a restaurant setting.

While servers can't force their customers to change, they do have the ability to serve (pun intended) as a positive influence for co-workers and customers alike. In this book, we intend to do just that: provide advice, along with true anecdotes, that will encourage you to become an upbeat, optimistic, and energetic server who makes the world a brighter place. In the last chapter, we identify seven of the most challenging customer types you are likely to encounter and show you how to successfully and gracefully deal with them. Our mission is to help you make your customers' experience delightful and become a role model and inspiration to your fellow co-workers.

We speak from rich—and sometimes painful—experience throughout these pages. Jim, Patrick, and Michael waited tables for decades. Brady, our illustrator, waited tables as well. Combined, we have logged 4,528 million hours serving folks in restaurants, and our experience ranges from being corporate restaurant trainers to being honored as "Waiter of the Year, 1997."

During our years as servers, we shamelessly made fun of clueless customers we waited on and raged over the occasional unbearable patron. But we were also learning so much: how to deal with the difficult people, how to spot a Stiff (and mentally prepare for the inevitable low tip!), and how to keep our sanity in the process. Though we had all taken notes, told stories, and mentioned the need for a book about this business, our efforts at creating anything tangible never really took off. Life happened to the three of us, and our ideas were shelved . . . until one day Jim—who is now a lawyer—read a book about making a difference in the world. The book noted that everyone, no matter his or her background or level of education, has at least one book brewing inside of them. Jim wondered what he could write about. John Grisham he is not; plus, he had no desire to write about being a lawyer, the law, or the legal process.

And then it hit him.

He could write about waiting tables! No one writes about the experiences of being a server, even though there are loads of interesting situations that occur in a restaurant that are universal to servers and waitstaff. He knew if he revisited his notes from years ago, he could transform them into a book. As the book took shape, it became clear that servers tend to deal with major issues when working in the restaurant business, and that is what he honed in on for the purposes of this book.

Now, the point of writing the book in the first place was to make a positive impact on the world and give back some of what we had been blessed to receive. But how could a book about restaurants fulfill those goals? The answer is a simple one: in addition to teaching you, as a server, how to become even better at what you do, Jim also committed to giving back by donating the first 10 percent of the book's revenue to charity.

Convinced that the book could be a vehicle to accomplish this bigger goal of giving back, Jim assembled a team to assist him with his mission:

Enter Michael Rathke

Not only is Michael a solid server with an amazing sense of humor, but he also happens to be an incredibly giving person by nature. When Michael learned about the project's philanthropic purpose, he immediately pledged his help. Still, the two knew they needed someone to review their rough draft once completed further and smooth it out. In search of a grammarian—who might happen to have experience in a restaurant—Michael and Jim didn't have to look far . . .

Enter Patrick Caldwell

Patrick is a lawyer today, but before that he was a waiter. He too liked the philanthropic component of this project and gladly edited the prose. More importantly, Patrick saw the bigger picture: he pointed out that the underlying principles of these steps could become a true contribution to society, even if only practiced by a small handful of people. All the book needed now was someone who could really help bring it to life . . .

Enter Brady Smith

Brady is an artist and actor who has been drawing since he could hold a crayon. Best of all, the artistic Brady also has bartending experience. As we continued to work on the book, we would always anxiously await his emails with the next installment of illustrations. We often laughed out loud when we received those comical illustrations, and we hope you'll do the same.

Establishing the team and creating this book was truly a labor of love, and the writing flowed very easily and naturally – which reaffirms our philosophy that when you focus on others more than yourself, good stuff naturally happens.

The ideas presented in this book are within the context of serving others in a restaurant setting, so naturally this book will be tremendously helpful for servers, restaurateurs, and restaurant managers wanting to up their game. At the same time, it is our earnest conviction that these themes provide a framework for daily living for any human being that, when followed, will at least in some small way make the world a better place.

TEN STEPS TO BECOMING A TOP SERVER

Everyone eats and most everyone eats at a restaurant from time to time. It would be wise for the customer to always remember that the people doing the serving are usually the last people to see the customer's meal before she eats it, and for the server to remember that the customer wants the server to make the customer's life better, not worse. This is why we've created the following chapters to hopefully develop an understanding of both sides of the restaurant experience.

While the following steps are primarily for the server in a restaurant, a customer who reads and learns these will know when she receives objectively bad service rather than service that just seems to stink, simply because the rest of her day has stunk. As for servers, however, they know and understand that there is a direct correlation between service and tips, at least there is supposed to be. The way it should work is that better service equals better tips. Servers also know and understand that it does not always work out this way. But there are less obvious reasons for a server to read these steps too.

The better the server, the better the shift and sections the server will work. Restaurant management wants their best people in the best spots at the best time. Applying these steps for success will make the server better, which should translate into more money, but also, as we will explain, better opportunities.

In addition to helping you make more money, these success tips can help you make more of yourself, too. If a server does not realize or understand how to fully take advantage of the fertile training ground for life that being a server provides, that server may find that waiting table stops being something she does part-time after school and becomes a full time career. And for a server who cannot master these guidelines, that full time career will likely remain a source of pain instead of pride.

The service industry is a decent and respectable profession. There is zero shame in the serving game. And a lot of people love the lifestyle of a waiter, and we understand and respect that as well. However, we think that these career-oriented servers are the minority. The majority of servers hope that waiting tables is a stepping stone in life towards whatever their plan takes them, assuming they have a plan. In their minds, they aspire to do something different, something bigger, better, and brighter. Understanding these 10 steps will help those aspiring servers achieve their aspirations.

People who can master the basics of good service can go on to lead and succeed. Fundamental to being a successful server is an understanding of people. As Dale Carnegie said in *How to Win Friends and Influence People*, quoting Owen D. Young: "People who can put themselves in the place of other people, who can understand the workings of their minds, need never worry about what the future has in store for them." This is what this book is all about—understanding people—to treat them how they want to be treated. The server who follows the concepts in this book while waiting tables will make bigger and better tips. Of that we are certain. The server who applies the principles that underpin the steps to life outside of the restaurant will be headed toward achieving whatever it is they believe they can achieve. This is where the real and true success comes into play. We hope you are encouraged to read on and are enthusiastic about doing so now.

We understand that every server has his or her own style. The steps are in no way meant to cage the server's own personal "Flair," as creatively coined in the movie Office Space in reference to required pins on aprons. Rather, these ideas in this book are meant to ensure that the server has the tools she needs to understand and provide exceptional, professional service.

Better servers equals better restaurants, which equals better places to work, which equals more money being made by the servers, which might equal more money being saved and spent in the economy, which makes everyone happier. And it also might mean that people are being kind and civil to one another more often, which would be nothing short of fantastic.

The customer is always right. This maxim needs repeating. The customer is always right.

STEP 1:

THE CUSTOMER IS ALWAYS RIGHT

*Your most unhappy customers are
your greatest source of learning.*

—Bill Gates

*Our DNA is as a consumer company—for that individual
customer who's voting thumbs up or thumbs down.
That's who we think about. And we think that our job is
to take responsibility for the complete user experience.*

And if it's not up to par, it's our fault, plain and simple.

—Steve Jobs

Regardless if a customer behaves in ways unimaginable, the customer is still the customer and should be treated like royalty. This is just the way it is and all servers need to embed this concept into their subconscious minds.

There are only two exceptions to this e. If the customer 1) becomes abusive to the server or staff, or 2) continually disrupts the dining experience of other patrons. If these situations are in play, immediately get the manager's attention so that he or she can deal with the unruly customer and you can continue to serve all other customers professionally. As soon as the less-than-pleasant customers have left the parking lot, immediately go into the walk-in refrigerator in the kitchen and scream or do whatever else you need to do to get over it and move on with your shift. Do not under any circumstance complain about a crummy table to another table. Remember, the non-offending customer is always right, and the customers you might complain to know this to be true, too.

STEP 2:
G.R.A.T.U.I.T.Y

I wasn't a good waitress, but I was told that I was very nice and charming, so people liked me anyway.

—Jennifer Aniston

I started in the restaurant business at the age of 19 as a waitress.

I loved the atmosphere and the camaraderie of the restaurant business. I loved not having to go to an office. I loved making people happy.

—Anne Burrell

The authors' serving skills have been honed for decades of combined service as waiters and bartenders in various restaurants. During the course of our respective careers in the service industry and through trial and error, we have stumbled upon a foolproof method for providing exceptional service and getting great tips. Our method can be easily remembered because it forms an acronym: G.R.A.T.U.I.T.Y. While there are no doubt other effective methods of providing exceptional, professional service, this system has worked well for us over the years and we are certain that if you use it properly you will land bigger tips.

G.R.A.T.U.I.T.Y stands for:

- Greet and welcome
- Request drink orders
- Advise of specials and up-sell
- Take food order
- [be] Useful and Unobtrusive while the food is being prepared
- Inquire if all is well
- Take away plates and up-sell again
- Yield after payment

This process is not ironclad and requires the server to be flexible and able to adapt if a table throws her a curve ball. Every table is different, of course, but almost all of them will be well served if you follow these guidelines. With that in mind, let us go over each of the steps in detail.

GREET AND WELCOME

The server must greet the table within thirty seconds. If the server responsible for the table is indisposed and not able to get there in time, another server should greet and welcome the table. This first step is critical to delivering solid service and requires a smile from the server conveying a sincere appreciation of the fact that the customer chose to be there. All preconceived notions and stereotypes as to the type of diners or the tip that will ultimately be awarded must be expelled. Everyone deserves to be treated equally without being the subject of a server's value judgment. Remember, they have options. Why thirty seconds? Thirty seconds is enough time for the guests to take off their coats and settle into their seats. Within a half-minute after sitting down, customers will expect to be able to start asking for things, typically drinks, but sometimes their first question is, "Where is the rest room?" Showing up within that critical thirty seconds gives the customer the earliest possible opportunity to ask for your help if they need anything urgently. Most customers won't need anything all that immediately, but keeping a customer waiting if that customer does have an urgent request will start the whole experience off on a sour note. You can avoid that problem altogether if you simply check in within thirty seconds.

And remember, you cannot always tell someone's internal state from their external appearance. The cheerful looking fellow at table six might have just been fired and is now cheerfully considering jumping in front of a train. The sour-faced gal in the booth by the window may turn out to be just as irritated as you over the latest episode of your favorite television show, and will end up being your best friend. Obviously, not many of your tables will be soul mates-in-waiting or secret tragedies about to happen absent your fortuitous intervention. But yours might be the only smile that customer sees in a week—and this is true for a lot more of your guests than you might expect. Make that smile count!

REQUEST DRINK ORDERS

The first thing the server needs to do after greeting and welcoming the table is to request drink orders. Suggesting a specialty drink or two may be appropriate here if the drink is worthy of your recommendation. Obviously, if the table asks any questions, answer them accurately. After taking the order, go prepare the drinks (or get them started) and allow the table to review the menu outside of your presence. Give them space, but keep an eye on them, too.

There are two points in the table life cycle where the customers are their most impatient. The most impatient point is when they are ready to leave and want to pay the check. The next most impatient point is immediately after they've decided what they want to order. If you can, try to return right after they've decided, but not before. If you're sharp you'll notice some common behaviors, such as closing the menu, putting the menus off to one side, or looking up and around the restaurant to try to catch your attention. Reducing the time your guests wait for you to serve them will make up for a lot of mistakes. We'll cover this in more detail later.

For now, the only exception to returning to the table before they're ready is to deliver their previous order, that is, the drinks.

ADVISE OF SPECIALS AND UP-SELL

When you return with the table's drinks, advise the table of the specials and ask if the table would like to start out with an appetizer. The table may have already asked while you were taking drink orders, but if not, this is when to handle it for sure. Be specific in asking by perhaps suggesting your favorite: "Have you guys tried our chips and queso? It's really good." If they want an appetizer, ask if they want you to go ahead and put that order into the kitchen now or if they want to order the whole meal while you are there.

We understand the restaurant's desire for you, the server, to up-sell like mad. The restaurant would always prefer customers to order more and more stuff. There is a delicate balance between gently nudging customers into an item and becoming a nuisance.

If you find yourself sounding like you're trying to talk them into the restaurant equivalent of an undercoating or extended warranty, you're probably over the line.

As you're probably already aware if you've waited tables longer than ten minutes, there are some customers who are aggravated by any hint of up-selling, especially the canned, cornpone suggestions in many typical restaurant manuals. Over time, you will get a better feel for how customers want to be advised of specials. Most people can tell if you really think the queso is good or if you're just trying to pad the check. The more sincerely you consider what they might actually enjoy, instead of simply speaking unwanted advertisements at your customers, the more they'll appreciate your input.

Remember, the key is delivering the best service to the customer, making the customer the happiest, not the restaurant. You have responsibilities to the restaurant, of course, but try to keep the customer's satisfaction as your highest priority while working within your duties to your employer. A happy customer makes for a happy restaurant anyway.

TAKE FOOD ORDER

Take the food order from the table whenever your guests are ready to give it. Do not rush the table and do not pester them about it. On the other hand, do not make the table wait to order either. Exercise some common sense and discretion here. If the menus were once up and are now down and it looks like they are ready to order, go for it. Otherwise, have them let you know when they are ready to order and then make yourself available to get it as soon as they are ready to give it. This point is especially important: WRITE DOWN THE ORDER. Even if you just decided to pick up a shift for old-time's sake, as you were passing through town on your way to the World Memory Masters Championships, WRITE IT DOWN. This serves the obvious purpose of preventing you from forgetting the order, but it also serves a second purpose. This simple step helps the customers feel better about the order. You may in fact be a genius, but to the customer, you're some guy in an apron who is about to forget he wants mayo with his fries. Help the customer trust you by writing it down.

Once you've taken the order, immediately give it to the kitchen however the restaurant is set up to do that. If you do not, you may get busy and forget. It happens, but it is nevertheless completely your fault if it does. So, enter the order instantly after you take it. And get it to the kitchen in a way that allows whoever ends up getting the food to your table to know who is eating what, if your restaurant has a system in place for that function.

BE USEFUL BUT UNOBTRUSIVE WHILE THE FOOD IS BEING PREPARED

Give the table some space while you wait for the table's order to be ready. Fill up drinks and reload other freebies like tortilla chips or rolls and tend to the table's requests, if any, during this time. Otherwise, if you are not doing this, make yourself available but scarce.

There are two aspects to this. First, you can prevent a lot of pain by keeping things tidy and stocked during your idle time. Keeping your (and your co-worker's) tables topped off on coffee, other drinks, etc., will prevent you from having to triage between similarly angry customers who are out of water. As you gain experience, you can learn to read the rhythm of the table, noticing, for example, that the guy in booth three will sit with a full soda for twenty minutes, then down it all in one gulp.

The second aspect of this is momentum. Waiting tables is hard work and your body will seem naturally want to rest at every opportunity. If you give in to this temptation and lean idly against the wall whenever you are not actively fulfilling an order, it will become increasingly more difficult to get up when you're called. That temptation will be easily visible in your posture and mannerisms, both by the manager and, more importantly, the customers. Your customers won't be able to distinguish the difference between being tired and being annoyed. They can only see the grimace you make as you push off the server station. Humans naturally interpret such gestures as responsive to their own input—don't let your guests catch you looking like leaving your wall perch to come to their table is a huge hassle for you. Staying busy with other tasks is the best way to avoid this problem.

INQUIRE IF ALL IS WELL

When the food is delivered, either by you or a food runner, ask the table if everything came out as ordered. If they need something else, go and get it, even if it is not your table and you were just the food runner. Address any concerns the table may have. Then, give the table a minute or so to taste what they ordered and then return to the table and ask if all is well. If all is well, be useful but unobtrusive again. If not, take care of whatever needs to be taken care of and then let the table eat in peace.

This step will save you a lot of headaches and help prevent customers from gaming the "comp" system. It prevents the customers from complaining that the food was not to their satisfaction or not what they ordered—after they have eaten everything but the parsley. If you check their order twice, giving them plenty of time to notice anything unsatisfactory, you will give both yourself and the restaurant the chance to fix it and prevent the customer from trying to cheat the restaurant. As you would probably guess, people who try to get their meal comp'd after they've eaten it are not big tippers. Most of your guests will be good, honest people—this step helps keep honest people honest.

TAKE AWAY PLATES AND UP-SELL

Pre-bus your tables. If someone is done with a plate, remove it pronto. No one wants to sit with an empty plate in their lap. But be mindful of the other guests. Use your best judgment as to whether or not you should pre-bus Mr. Hoover's empty plate when his companions have only just lifted their forks.

In any case, no plates should be left on the table when you drop the check. After the table is cleared, ask if dessert or coffee is in order. If so, repeat the previous two steps. If not, drop the check as soon as possible and then remove yourself from the equation. Return to pick up payment as soon as you notice it's ready. The basic idea in this step is to clear away the plates and other things that prevent the guests from relaxing and enjoying their time with their companions for a bit. For business lunches, this is often when the guests want to be able to use the table to share documents or look at their smartphones together. If you can clear away the plates quickly (but not before they've finished eating!), you will help your guests make the most of their time in the restaurant.

Especially in business lunches, one or more of the guests may be nervously waiting for an opportunity to broach a sensitive subject, and the post-meal happy glow of contentment is a good time to do that. You can help your guests by clearing away the plates and then staying out of their way as much as you can. You want to avoid interrupting an important question or discussion, especially over low-value requests. The guest would much rather have his companion agree to let him handle the Johnson account, for example, than get another three ounces of water from you.

This is so common, though, that it has become a staple of romantic comedies—just as the hapless protagonist is about to propose marriage, the waiter shows up wanting to talk about dessert specials. This can be funny in movies, but it's really hard on your tips. If your guests look like they're in the middle of an important conversation, give them a little space. They'll let you know they're ready for you to return when one of them picks up and looks at the bill.

YIELD

Once the credit card slip for signature or cash change is placed on the table, yield. If something needs to be signed, leave a pen that works. Do not pocket the tip from the table until everyone who was sitting there has left. Do not continue to serve unless the table requests something. Make sure to say "thank you" at least twice: once when you pick up payment and then again when the table is leaving, but always before you gather your tip.

This is something of an extension of the above step, with the understanding that the guests are now preparing to leave the restaurant. If you can help them make that easier, please feel free. But you should also avoid seeming like you are actively pushing them out the door. It may be especially difficult to relax around closing time, but do your best. A good guest will appreciate that they came in late and will often add a little extra to your tip so long as you're not making them pay by rushing them out the door.

G.R.A.T.U.I.T.Y is a straightforward, flexible approach to service. If you follow these guidelines, your tips will improve overall, even though not every guest will tip well. While the rest of the steps have additional applicability outside the restaurant, when practice G.R.A.T.U.I.T.Y, you will strengthen your people skills in all other areas of your life. It is impossible not to.

STEP 3:
TIP-OUT CHEERFULLY

Real generosity is doing something nice
for someone who will never find out.

—Frank A. Clark

In theory, the tip-out performs the same function that gratuities are supposed to serve, that is, motivating the support staff to provide excellent support to the waiters. In practice, this is almost never the case. Instead, many restaurants take advantage of the tipping culture to reduce the labor cost the restaurant bears in hiring non-waiter employees, allowing no discretion on the part of the waiters on tipping-out. Just as the restaurant has shifted some of the burden of paying you, the server, to the restaurant customer, the restaurant has also shifted some of the burden of paying the bartender and the busboy to you, too. And as the case may be with tips for waiters from their guests, not all waiters receive excellent service or tip properly within their own ranks.

Unlike the guests, however, tipping-out the support staff is not optional and usually wholly unrelated to the "service" you receive from them. Some restaurants require the servers to tip-out a certain percentage of sales; others ask for a pre-determined, fixed amount.

When a certain percentage is required, some servers often tip-out reluctantly because they feel that the value of the assistance rendered does not equate to the amount of the required tip-out. This is particularly true on busy shifts, when it seems like the busboy spent more time on his phone in the walk-in than clearing plates. When tipping-out is not strictly required, the same sort of server may consider not tipping-out at all or low balling the tip-out, basically stiffing the help. Both approaches are misguided.

We think you should tip-out cheerfully and in full, after every shift, regardless of whether it is required, and subject to the same standards customers use to tip you. That is, assuming you received "standard, non-terrible" service, you should tip the full amount expected. In the event you don't receive "standard, non-terrible" service, you have fewer options than the customer, but you still have some options.

First, keep in mind that you are not the only person being served by a troublesome support staffer. If the busboy really did spend most of the shift goofing off, the other waiters and the manager noticed. Before taking any irrevocable action (like complaining to the manager), try to get a sense from the other waiters whether the service you received was as bad as you think it was. We are all vulnerable to having bad days, and on bad days, everything everyone does stinks. If you're having a bad day, the busboy could be replacing your dirty dishes with gold coins and it would still be irritating. To make sure you're accurately reading the situation, ask your fellow servers if they had similar problems. This won't solve all support staff issues, but it will prevent imaginary issues from blossoming into real ones.

Second, depending on the relationship you have with the particular support person, you can consider talking to them privately. Find out whether there is a good reason why, for example, your tables aren't getting bussed well or you've had to send every drink back. Sometimes folks just aren't at the top of their game. You've had shifts, we're sure, where it seemed you dropped more plates than delivered. Give yourself the opportunity to show some compassion to the support staffers. Both of you will be better for it.

Finally, if neither of the above approaches clarifies the issue, it's time to talk to the boss. You're the customer in this situation, but you're something of a captive consumer. Because both of your jobs are under management's responsibility, you will want to exercise all of your tact in complaining about the support staff.

The most important guideline here is to be sure to complain about the behavior, not the person. And if possible, offer a suggestion as to how to fix it. If you can think of how management might address the problem and can present a solution at the same time as your complaint, the manager will be very grateful for the input. If, instead, you merely show up and complain about "that smelly dirtbag" who "didn't do anything" all shift, you're not giving management much to work with. Worse, in the manager's mind, you're now a problem the manager has to solve. It's not fair, but that's human psychology.

We understand that it won't always be easy to tip-out cheerfully.

But please try to remember that the "help" is essential to providing a top-notch experience for your tables, and they expect tip-outs, just as you expect your tables to leave you a gratuity. Doing this will only help you, despite the short-term hit to your cash-in-hand.

This is how it works. If you cheerfully tip-out the support staff and reward them for their assistance, you will get more and better assistance from them in the future, thereby allowing you to give more and better service to your tables. For instance, your tables will be cleaned first, your table's beers will be poured first, and your food will be delivered to your tables first. So, in addition to your stellar handling of the table, getting first-class service from the support staff will allow you to give first-class service to your tables and, consequently, get first-class tips. Besides, you may be in the position of getting tipped-out yourself at some point and would certainly like to receive the same treatment.

STEP 4:

IT'S NOT ABOUT YOU

When you're holding people's attention, I feel
you must give them high-quality ingredients.
They deserve nothing but your best.

And if they need information, get it, cross-check
it, and try to be right. Do not waste their time;
do not enjoy the ego trip of being onstage.

—Henry Rollins

A recent trend is that servers have generally become more friendly and personable. The thinking seems to be that guests would never under tip a friend, and so the more friendly the waiter, the less likely the waiter will get stiffed. This reasoning does have some appeal.

However, in our experience, overly friendly waiters tend to receive fewer tips than simply cheerful and professional waiters. The reason is similar to the "Uncanny Valley" in robotics. Android researchers discovered that people respond rather naturally to robots that either are clearly machines or extremely lifelike. But there is a sharply negative reaction to robots that look like people, and yet don't quite get all the way to lifelike. This is the Uncanny Valley—it's a gut-level response to a weirdly human face.

People are much more comfortable interacting with complete strangers or close friends than with uncertain acquaintances. Even grumpy waiters are easier to interact with than overly friendly waiters. We believe that the leap from "friendly" to "friend" is too easy to misread. And tips are sparse in the Uncanny Valley.

Unless you know that someone came to the restaurant specifically to see you and to eat, it's safe to assume that the guests are not at your table on a social call, so do not make the experience about you. Instead, the customer usually wants to visit with the people sitting at that table and would rather not be disturbed. Accordingly, follow G.R.A.T.U.I.T.Y, and when you do need to chat with the table, the verbal exchange should not be about you. Keep in mind that the table will let you know if it's in the mood for a chat, so be sure to listen for those cues.

If a table wants to visit with you, by all means be pleasant and engage the guests in light conversation. However, there are certain topics that should be off limits—even if the customer asks. Obviously, the standard rules of etiquette apply and you should avoid politics, religion, etc. Additionally, never, ever talk about your money woes or financial problems, none of which are the customer's responsibility. Talking about money to a person whom you expect to give you money makes for an awkward and unwelcome tension between the table and server. As soon as you leave the table, the folks sitting at it are likely saying out loud or to themselves: "He told us that to try and get a bigger tip." This is uncomfortable. The table does not like being manipulated and such pandering usually does not help the server anyway. Stiffing falls into this category as well. No table wants to hear about how the last table stiffed you. Professional servers want to be tipped because they provide extraordinary service, not because a table felt sorry for them. Be professional.

As a general rule, then, complaining about anything is forbidden, especially complaining about the restaurant, other servers, or the kitchen. Your job as a server is to make the customer's life better, not worse, if only for a moment. You are a representative of the restaurant, and it is part of your job to put the restaurant in the best light possible. Fussing about how lame it is to work there, or about another server who stole your table, or how the kitchen brought its B game that day does not advance this ball.

Complaining in such a fashion is unpleasant to listen to and makes the customer perhaps wish they chose some other less lame place to eat. So do not do it. Moreover, how tired you are, how awful your roommate is, how much your head hurts, or how your girlfriend just left you because you complain all the time is none of the table's business and they do not want to know about it. Keep your life's drama to yourself. Your customers have problems of their own to deal with and do not need to tackle your drama, too. Remember, it's about them; it's not about you.

This step can also adapt quite easily beyond the walls of the restaurant. We all want friends to lean on during tough times, but nobody likes a chronic complainer. If you practice enduring and overcoming the slights and unfairness that regularly assail you in the restaurant environment, your overall attitude will change in remarkable ways. Giving in to complaining corrodes your character and keeps your focus on everything that is wrong in your life.

Worse, it does so in a way that retains all of the pain of what's wrong, without allowing for any reflection on how to improve the situation. Habitual complaining will reinforce every bad habit you have, eventually resulting in a psychological state known as "learned helplessness." Once established, learned helplessness is as difficult to cure as foot fungus.

To see the difference, try this experiment. On your next shift, endeavor to say nothing negative about anything or anyone, even indirectly. It will feel weird at first, but we think you'll be astonished at how you feel at the end of the shift.

STEP 5:

WAITING TABLES IS A TEAM SPORT

Teamwork is the ability to work together toward a common vision.

The ability to direct individual accomplishments toward organizational objectives. It is the fuel that allows common people to attain uncommon results.

—Andrew Carnegie

Teamwork is absolutely essential for exceptional service, which is absolutely essential to generating repeat customers—and this is the goal of all restaurants. Servers that scratch each other's backs always provide better service. Management knows this and looks for it. The customers notice, too.

What do we mean by teamwork? Here are some examples of how you can be a better team player. Greet a table that has not been greeted yet, even if it is not in your section. Grab an empty plate from a table, even if it is not your table. Refill drinks, even if the empties are not at your table. Run food, even if it is not food for one of your tables. Ask if anyone needs help when you are slow. If you do these kinds of things, you are a true team player and you will reap the benefits. You will, without question, get noticed by the management and have as many shifts as you can handle. You will also surely begin to notice that your customers are being taken care of for you, too—they have been greeted with their drink order taken, their food is delivered, their drinks are full, their empty plates have been removed, and so on. What goes around truly comes around in the restaurant business.

There are other aspects of teamwork for servers in addition to helping with each other's tables. Being a solid team player means showing up for your shift on time or calling in, well in advance, if you absolutely can't make it in to work. Not showing up for work is bad, not showing up and not calling to say you are not showing up is despicable. There is likely nothing more infuriating for a restaurant staff than the "no-call-no-show." If you miss and do not call in beforehand you need to either be in jail or dead—and only one of these is remotely acceptable. You would not dream of keeping your "real" job if you failed to show up to work without providing some sort of notice and explanation. (And you better have a darn good excuse if you want to stay employed.) The exact same thing is true when you are a server in a restaurant.

And as a true team player, and if you can manage it, take on a shift for another server if he needs a shift covered. At some point in the future you will likely need to rearrange your schedule, too, and you'll want the same team-spirited assistance in covering one of your shifts. It is never a bad thing to be thought of as the most helpful and professional server on staff. Indeed, every table wants to be waited on by the best server. The best server is always a solid team player— and he or she might as well be you.

STEP 6:

YOU DON'T HAVE TO GO HOME BUT YOU CAN'T STAY HERE

I think when things linger, that's when they become a distraction.

I don't want any distractions.

—Derek Jeter

There is a peculiar custom among servers and other restaurant staff—they stick around after work or hang out at the restaurant on their days off or after they finish a shift. It is truly bizarre. Non-restaurant employees do not generally swing by the office to hang out when they are not working, or loiter around the cubicles visiting with their colleagues until everyone gets around to leaving after a day's work (unless they are waiting on traffic to die down or something). Non-restaurant folk typically stay far away from their workplace on their days off and get the heck out of the office when their work is done for the day. Not so with servers.

Servers will finish a lunch shift and then maybe order a meal or hang out for a while before leaving. Or servers will come to the restaurant to eat or drink on their days off and to visit with their co-workers. It happens all the time. Much of this strange behavior stems from the food discount servers get—it's just cheaper sometimes for them to eat where they work. Some of it probably comes from the natural collegiality that grows between people in the restaurant business. This is one of the best parts of working in the service industry and we don't begrudge anyone wanting to savor it.

We understand and we know that servers would not work at a restaurant for very long if they didn't hit it off with the other staff. It is much easier for a server to migrate to a different restaurant if she does not get along with the other servers than it is for a non-restaurant employee to move to a different company if she dislikes her co-workers. This is because restaurants are always on the lookout for experienced staff, whereas most other job opportunities require a formal resumé, sometimes lengthy interview processes, and time-consuming reference checks.

Working with people you hate is painful, to put it mildly. The fact that servers in restaurants notoriously enjoy working together is immensely important and cannot be overvalued. Add to this the discount you get as part of your compensation when you eat where you work is another perk of the job. You should take advantage of it—there is no doubt about it.

But remember, the restaurant where you work is your office, not your playground. There is a balance between enjoying the companionship of your peers and lingering underfoot when they're busy. Simply put, make sure your off-hours presence at the restaurant is not distracting to the other servers and staff or the customers.[1] So, after your shift, you do not have to go home but you shouldn't stay there.

---

1   It is worth noting that a large portion of this book was written in a Starbucks. On every single occasion when we were there working on this project—no joke, every single time—a different one of the off-duty baristas came in, ordered a drink, made a scene, and then left. We are talking 100% of the time. It was more entertaining than it was distracting and usually happened within the first fifteen minutes or so. It must be the free drinks, but we still think this is insane.

STEP 7:

PLEASE DON'T TRY TO BE FUNNY WHEN YOU AREN'T

I think being funny is not anyone's first choice.

—Woody Allen

We readily admit that the subject of this step may get under our skin more than it should. Actually, non-funny people trying to be funny may not bother the general population at all. As for us, however, we think being hanged, drawn, and quartered is preferable to listening to a non-funny person endeavor to be funny. In fact, non-funniness has been known to cause us physical pain and nausea. Accordingly, we had no choice but to include a step about non-funny servers trying to be funny.

Funny people know they are funny. How do they know? In two ways, typically. First, they have been told they are funny. A lot. Second, they routinely make people laugh genuinely, not a fake sympathy laugh (which are always obvious, by the way—even to the non-funny person). If you have never been told you are funny—you are not. If you do not crack people up all the time and occasionally make then bend over in a full-fledged belly laugh—you are not funny. Funny people are told they are funny and bring about belly laughs frequently. You can still be a stellar server, even if you are not a funny person; loads of people are. You can no doubt capitalize on your many other assets and should. Just don't try to be funny—it never ends well.

One typical, non-funny go-to move is the pretending to be unfriendly or unhelpful shtick. It goes something like this:

Customer: "Can I please have some more ice?"
Server: "I don't know, can you?"

Writing such an exchange is just as painful as listening to it. The proper response to such a request is "Yes, right away." Funny people know this, non-funny people seem not to.

Here's another example:

Customer: "Can we please have some more bread?"
Server: "No."

Obviously, everyone knows the server is trying to be funny and is not being serious when denying the request for more bread. Equally obvious is how not funny it is. Just say "Yes, of course" and get them more bread.

If you are not funny, please, please do not try to be. Just be super-knowledgeable, pleasant, and useful instead. Providing exceptional, professional service does not require joking around with your tables. And providing professional service is why you are there and why the restaurant hired you.

Naturally, this may sound elitist and a bit off-putting, especially if you are not funny. More generally, this step is about being sincere and authentic—being who you truly are. We are bombarded with examples of the "ideal" personality, especially in advertisements. The "funny" guy is one such ideal.

This step is our humble antidote to that ideal. Many, many people spend much of their lives trying to contort their natural personality to something beyond their reach. We believe you will be happier and more successful if you are better able to see who you really are, and to be that person.

Of course, we're not advocating you give up on your dreams. If you aren't funny but your lifelong dream is to be a stand-up comedian, please, go forth with gusto! But recognize that your talents may lie elsewhere. This isn't an argument for choosing a more attainable dream, but instead, encouragement to be honest with yourself. If you're not funny, you're going to have to work a whole lot harder to be a stand-up.

Be honest with yourself. If you're not funny, find out what you are naturally good at. Maybe you have a knack for putting together the perfect wine with dessert. Maybe you are able to juggle six big tops' worth of trays at once without dropping so much as a crumb. Get great at what you're naturally good at and you will never be interested in being funny again if you aren't already funny.

STEP 8:

HONESTY IS THE BEST POLICY

Mistakes are always forgivable, if one has the courage to admit them.

—Bruce Lee

M indful honesty is always the best policy, regardless of where you work. Most servers are human. Humans make mistakes from time to time. What separates the professional servers from the amateurs is how the server handles those mistakes. There is no mistake a server can make that is so severe it would justify the sacrificing of her character and integrity by lying about the mistake to cover it up. No tip is worth lying about a mistake. In fact, it has been our experience that sincerity sells way better than dishonesty.

If you forget to put in an order and it delays the table in some way, be honest about it. If you were misinformed about a menu item, fess up. If you otherwise screwed up, tell the truth. Recently, a server presented Jim with a bill that did not list the to-go order he had given to the server midway through the meal. Rather than say that she forgot to put the order in and would rush the order out if he still wanted it, the server said, "I'm sorry; I brought you the wrong bill," and then returned moments later with a new bill that included the previously excluded item.

The server obviously got busy and forgot to get the to-go order to the kitchen, but rather than say so she made up a ridiculous excuse. Professionals do not need to do that and they know it. A professional would have been honest and Jim would have appreciated her honesty. Jim, of course, did not stiff the server, but the experience did provide a timely example of how to better handle a mistake by being honest. No mistake is meaningless if it offers a lesson, so be honest about screwing up and learn from it rather than lie about it.

One final point is worth mentioning here. There is a world of difference between "honesty" and "brutal honesty." So-called "brutal honesty" is a façade for cruelty. Telling people "how it is" is not proper if the whole point of telling them is to hurt them. Honesty in this case does not justify being a mean-spirited jerk. Mindful honesty also requires an element of discretion and kindness. In Jim's example above, it would have been wholly inappropriate for the waitress to say, for example, "I'm sorry—I forgot to put in the order because my methadone wore off and I'm distracted by the DWI charges I'm facing." Oof, now that would really be awkward. So be honest, but resist the temptation to overshare, and the urge to use honesty to justify being mean.

STEP 9:

PUT YOUR PHONE AWAY

You can start right where you stand and apply the habit of going the extra mile by rendering more service and better service than you are now being paid for.

—Napoleon Hill

S imply put, servers need to put down their smart phones while they are at work. Actually, we think servers should leave their phones in their cars or lockers. If someone needs to get in touch with the server they can call the restaurant in the case of an emergency.[2] Other than some exigent circumstance requiring a telephone call, there is absolutely no need for a cell phone during a shift. Servers are getting paid to serve, not to update their status and certainly

---

2   If we were writing this book fifteen years ago, we may have included a step prohibiting people from telephoning the restaurant wanting to chat with a server, especially during peak serving hours. This day and age with everyone having smart phones, we thought that a step on this would be a little dated. In any event, people should not be calling the restaurant wanting to talk to any staff member really ever, but particularly during prime serving hours, unless it is an emergency.

not to comment on their tables online. In fact, days before writing this step a woman was fired from a restaurant in Ohio for complaining on Facebook about the crummy tips she received. We guess the only silver lining in that story was that the server waited until after her shift to rant. Suffice it to say that, given what we know of the incident, we agree with the restaurant.

Under no circumstances is it appropriate for a server to discuss details of restaurant patrons online, including the tips they leave— even if it is a celebrity. The folks coming to eat at the restaurant did not agree to have the details of their experience broadcast over the World Wide Web and such conduct could even invite a lawsuit. You have been warned! What happens in the restaurant should stay in the restaurant, or it should at least stay offline.

It is simply impossible for a server to focus on providing exceptional service if a server is more interested in text messaging rather than on her tables, or posting something on Twitter rather than preparing for her shift. Moreover, a server carrying on conversations via text or any other means, or just staying updated on social media presents the very real possibility that the server may learn some "drama" that ultimately results in the immature server not being able to focus on the tasks and tables at hand. Finding out that your boyfriend posted something ill-advised on your roommate's wall can wait until your shift is over. Drama needs to be dropped at the door. Remove the temptation. Put your phone down and out of reach.

Aside from the fact that removing the temptation will improve your service, it will also help you learn to stay focused and fully present in the task at hand. Put more plainly, smart phones are creeping into every aspect of our lives. Every office is filled with workers trying to work in thirty-second bursts in between checking their e-mail, social media, etc. The result is that folks are finding it harder and harder to be where they are.

Survey your tables some time. See how many couples spend their dinner time playing with their phones instead of being present with each other. If you're even a little observant, in business lunches you can spot the nervous twitch of the phone-aholic, fondling his cell phone while pretending to listen to his companion. Remove the distraction of the smart phone from your shift and you will be amazed at how much life there is unfolding right before your eyes.

As with all the other steps, leaving your phone in your locker is training for being present in the rest of your life. As more and more people are consumed by their handheld marvels, people who are present and engaged are becoming more and more rare. If you are able to attend to the other people in your life who are as undistracted as you are with your restaurant customers, you will find those people appreciative beyond words.

STEP 10:

TREAT EVERY TABLE LIKE IT'S AN INTERVIEW

I was raised in the environment where it really wasn't about sittin' around dreaming all the time, it was about practicing and workin' really hard and if a dream ever came to you, you'd be prepared for that opportunity.

—Harry Connick, Jr.

While it's still "not about you," being a server is a profession and servers are expected to be professionals. Using G.R.A.T.U.I.T.Y and treating every table like it's an interview is the epitome of providing professional, exceptional service to a table. What do we mean by treating a table like it's an interview? It's simple. We mean do the things you would do if you wanted to land the job of your dreams and were lucky enough to be selected to interview for the job.

Before the interview you would (we hope):

- Be clean and without dirty hair and fingernails.
- Be knowledgeable and prepared to answer any question.
- Be dressed properly.
- Be confident.
- Be engaging.
- Be respectful and polite.
- Be thankful.
- Be noticeably happy to be there.
- Be on time.
- Be well rested, ready, and eager.

Nothing on the above list is beyond your ability, right? If you show up to each one of your tables exhibiting these positive qualities you will be the most requested server wherever you are working. Regrettably, most of the time servers do not demonstrate all of these traits. Maybe a few, and some more than others, but it is unusual for a server to show up with all of them, regularly demonstrating their commitment to excellence for each and every table. Too often servers instead show up to their tables unprepared and out of uniform, such as not knowing the specials or not having a pen. Or showing up to tables tired, groggy from the night before with the blue stamp from the all-night rave he went to still emblazoned on his hand and looking like he slept in his work shirt. Or being lazy—like when a server, relying on his memory, does not write down a table's order when the table is telling him what they would like to eat and drink. While the statistical calculation on this is still a work in progress, not writing down an order has to at least double the chances of whatever is ordered arriving at the table wrong or arriving at the wrong table. The server has a pen and he should use it—it's part of his uniform. A server not having a pen is like a movie theater not having popcorn. Every moviegoer in America expects to be able to buy popcorn if they want it, and every customer expects the server to have a pen (so they can borrow it).

The restaurant would rather not have this sort of server working there and the customer would rather wait on himself than have a server in this state. Servers also show up to tables with preconceived notions and stereotypes that in their mind foretell a crummy tip and miserable time. These thoughts must be expelled. Every table deserves to be treated equally and not subject to the server's value judgment.

These senseless servers are missing a concept that is one of the basic principles when it comes to working with the public: You can't really know whom you're dealing with—so never assume you do! In the restaurant/server business, you may not be waiting on your best friend, but you ARE waiting on someone else's best friend, so treat everyone equally and as you'd like to be treated.

To put it another way, the server usually has no idea about what station in life, position, or career the customer they are serving may enjoy. The patron could be the hiring manager for a company in a field of work that the server is keenly interested in exploring. Or perhaps the guest is the manager at a five-star restaurant always on the lookout to hire more exceptional servers who are notorious for killing it in tips. Maybe the patron is a future teacher or professor the server will have in one of the courses he is taking. Maybe the customer is a future spouse or partner. The possibilities are endless.

We are not suggesting that servers hand out their resumé or engage in self-promotion when they drop off the bill at every table. Nor are we suggesting that servers should constantly be on the lookout for bigger and better jobs and mindlessly migrate from one opportunity to another. However, consistently putting your best foot forward and treating every table like it's a job interview will result in maximum tips and may likely open doors that would otherwise remain firmly closed for the less committed, less exceptional, less professional server. Being the best at what you do always pays off. The best servers treat every table like it's an interview. Be the best.

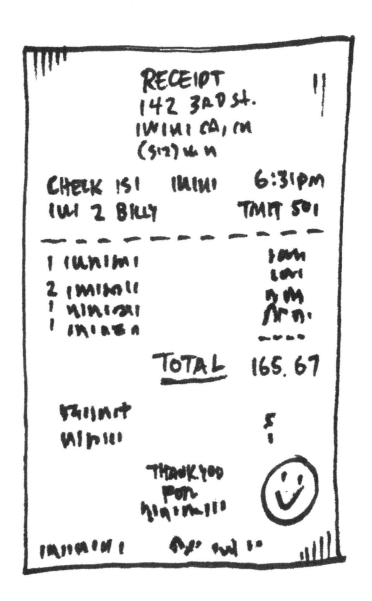

Those are our success steps for servers. We hope you will apply them while you are waiting tables, and we also hope that you apply them to whatever else you may choose to do when your waiting days are done. Remember, the better we treat others, the better our own lives will become. With your help we can start a dialogue about how to properly serve and be served in restaurants across the country—and maybe the globe!

THE SEVEN MOST ANNOYING CUSTOMER PERSONALITIES & HOW TO HANDLE THEM

No matter how long you've been in this business and no matter what type of restaurant setting you've worked in, you are bound to encounter annoying customers. After all, irritating and rude people need food too and would likely prefer that you bring it to them on a platter. Ranging from customers who think they are the center of the universe to customers who are oblivious, it is a certainty that you will encounter the full spectrum of restaurant customer types. In this chapter, we have identified the seven most common and frustrating ones:

- The Complainer
- The Stiff
- The Freeloader
- The Customizer
- The Mess Maker
- The Noisy Table
- The Flagger

You may already be nodding your head, remembering that loud customer from last week or the messy patron from lunchtime today. We certainly empathize with your discomfort in dealing with these behaviors and people, and that's why we are also providing you with some ideas that work exceptionally well with even the most difficult diners. Though there's not always a single perfect solution that works every time, there are some simple steps you can take to navigate the waters of challenging customers. Let's begin with one of the most common and most irritating customers, the one who's never happy. This is the Complainer.

THE COMPLAINER

Certainly, restaurant-goers have legitimate complaints at times; however, if you have someone complaining about something small or insignificant, and that complaint leads to more and more small criticisms, then you are probably dealing with a Complainer. Complainers gripe about service being too slow, food being too hot or cold, where their table is located, and the noise level, just to name a few. Perhaps the best way to illustrate this personality type is to give you some real-life scenarios that typify Complainers' tactics:

- After being seated and waiting a brief time: "Oh, we finally got somebody here," or "Nice to finally get some service."
- Depending on where the table is located and even though the restaurant may be jammed packed with patrons: "Why are we sitting so close to the kitchen? Can't we get a better table?"
- When it's chilly or noisy: "It's freezing here! Our table

is right next to that vent," or, "Can't you tell them to quiet down?"

- While serving drinks and entrees: "Oh, where am I going to put all this food? I hope you have to-go boxes!" or "I can barely taste the alcohol in this. It's not very strong . . ."

Again, there is a fine line with this category of restaurant-goer, because some of those complaints may be legitimate. If the bill is incorrectly calculated, if the order was wrong, or if they waited for an hour to place their order after being seated, these are absolutely valid criticisms. However, a true Complainer will trot out multiple complaints in a very short time. In other words, it wouldn't just be the wait but it would be the noise . . . *and* the temperature . . . *and* the serving size. The complaints have a domino effect to them, and the Complainer will find anything and everything to criticize.

You'll also notice that Complainers have unreasonable time expectations. As a server, you might have five or six tables to wait on and you can't very well get everyone's drinks in fifteen seconds; however, the Complainer is clueless of this. Of course, this does not mean that servers should ignore the time it takes to bring out orders. They should be as prompt as possible, while still knowing that when serving multiple tables it's impossible to be everywhere at once. Sadly, the Complainers at a restaurant aren't very realistic when it comes to a server's time

One of the worst examples of a Complainer we have ever experienced occurred when a gentleman sat down, took out twenty one-dollar bills, and then said to the server, "This is all yours, as long as you do a good job." Then, each time something happened that wasn't to his satisfaction, he took a dollar or two off the table. By the time he left, only six out of that twenty dollars remained. Clearly, this is a manipulative type of Complainer who doesn't use his words but instead used those dollar bills to pick apart the service.

Dealing with Complainers

Though not pleasant to deal with, there are some steps you can take to deal with Complainers effectively, and it's easiest to remember the technique using the acronym "H.E.A.T.":

1. **Hear** what the Complainers are saying. As unreasonable as they may be, it is important to listen to what they are complaining about so you are aware of the issue.
2. **Empathize.** Put yourself in the customer's shoes, so to speak, and do your best to understand their feelings. Maybe this is a big occasion and the customer wants everything to be perfect, or maybe he or she is spending more money than usual on the food, so expectations are through the roof; regardless of what the case may be, trying to consider it from the customer's point of view may help you to feel more compassionate (and less annoyed).
3. **Apologize.** Even if you have nothing to do with the complaint—which is usually the case—apologize by letting the Complainer know that you are sorry he or she is upset. A simple "I'm so sorry to hear that, and I totally understand" can do the trick.
4. **Take action.** Try to do something that will either remedy the situation or at least lessen the tension. Maybe you can get the customer's table moved, maybe the air conditioning can be turned down a bit, or maybe it's something as simple as getting the

customer to smile.

For example, if a customer complains that his table is too close to the kitchen, you can use H.E.A.T. like this:

- Focus on the customer when he says, "I really don't like being close to the kitchen," and then . . .
- Empathize with him by communicating that you understand that it actually might be very loud, too warm, etc. when sitting right next to the kitchen.
- Apologize by saying, "I'm sorry about that, Sir."
- Take action: You could say, "Let me see what I can do," and then check to see if you can move the patron to another table. If not, return to the table, apologize again and consider ways to "make up for" it (comp a drink, give extra attention to the customer, etc.).

THE STIFF

Imagine this: it's almost closing time and you've been running from table to table all evening. Most customers have been great, and you've been paying particularly close attention to their needs. But everything comes to a screeching halt with one particular customer. Not only has he kept you running more than the rest, but he's also given you a tip so paltry you figure it must be a mistake. If not a mistake, an intentional slight.

If it was not a mistake then it was an intentional slight.

An encounter with a Stiff.

Spotting a Stiff is not easy, but they do give warnings as to the forthcoming goose egg of a tip. Typically, the Stiff may reveal his nature early on in the dining experience by asking loads of price-related questions: "How much is a bottle of beer? How much is this seafood special? Aren't happy hour prices good until seven?" Now, there is nothing wrong with price inquiries; it's understandable, and we do this, too! However, tons of questions may be an indicator that, when it's time to tip, this person is going to stiff you.

Along the same lines, Stiffs will try to get menu items cheaper by doing things like asking for lemons and extra sugar to *make* his or her own lemonade! Yes, it's true. We know from personal experience; in fact, one of our friends is guilty of this ridiculousness. He justifies it by saying he likes the taste better, but we think he likes the price more.

Perhaps one of the biggest tells that you're in the presence of the Stiff is the request to share a plate. Many patrons who split a meal will then proceed to load up on the food: "Can I have more salsa? More chips? More bread?" If they're hoarding the food *and* trying to save money in the process, chances are good that these customers are not going to suddenly become tip-happy at the end of their dinner.

While all of the aforementioned signs point to the possibility of dealing with Stiffs, we caution you not to prejudge your customers too harshly or too quickly. That's because sometimes there are cultural differences at play. Without sensitivity to this fact, you may mistakenly predict you've got a knowingly cheap customer on your hands, when in fact you do not.

For example, when working at a popular upscale Chinese restaurant, a server we knew noticed that many patrons from one particular ethnic group would invariably tip 10 percent. That was it. At first, the server thought maybe it was a fluke, but over time he reported that about 90 percent of the customers from this group tipped 10 percent—no more, no less. Rather than getting angry and judgmental, he realized that this was the norm for this group. Though it initially came across as insulting, once our friend considered the cultural difference, he learned not to take the low tip so personally and instead tried to upsell like crazy.

How to Deal with a Stiff

Even though *you* understand what goes on behind the scenes at a restaurant, many of your customers don't realize how much you depend on those tips and how hard you are working for them. So, of course, when a generous tip doesn't come your way, it's difficult. Fortunately, there are a few actions you can take when you're dealing with a Stiff.

First, avoid prejudgement. While the signs may be there, this doesn't automatically guarantee a low tip. There are no absolutes in this business. In fact, sometimes the customers that we were sure would stiff us ended up being the most generous tippers of the day. Yes, it's important to be aware of the red flags, but you may be pleasantly surprised in the end.

In the event that you *do* get stiffed, it is important to get it out of your system . . . but that does *not* mean chasing the customer outside so that you can fling the seventy-five-cent tip back at them! Here is a good example that illustrates this mistake. A few teenagers paid their forty-nine-dollar tab with a fifty-dollar bill, and the waiter followed them into the parking lot, handed them the change, and said, "Thanks, guys, I've got to pay the rent this week. I really appreciate it." As you can guess, that didn't go over well. After a few "Screw yous" from the teens, the waiter returned to the restaurant, empty-handed. Fortunately, he didn't get fired, even though his behavior would have warranted it.

So, how can you clear the air when you're upset? Simply acknowledging your feelings and sharing how you feel with your server friends is an effective method. Not only will they understand where you're coming from, but most will also respond empathetically to your situation. Servers love to commiserate with other servers.

Then, once you've given yourself a moment to vent, do your best to get back into the groove at work. Keeping yourself busy allows you to avoid fixating on the difficult customer. Plus, it allows you to focus on other customers who may very willing to reflect their gratitude with a generous tip!

Finally, understand that most customers simply tip what they tip and that getting stiffed now and then is going to happen and is simply a cost of doing business. And it is not always an indication of your performance as a server. In other words, some people have a percentage in mind that they always use, no matter the service, and in some cases this is zero. Some tippers are taking notes the whole time—adding and subtracting from your tip based on every positive and negative thing they perceive you are doing. That's just how they are. It doesn't matter who the server is. Whether you agree with it or not, once you realize that most tipping amounts (and the "philosophies" behind those tips) were established before you ever stepped up to the table, it will be easier for you to not take bad tips personally and just continue doing a great job. That said, if low or no tips begin to become the rule rather than the exception, you may need to think about another profession or really try to hone your skills a server.

THE FREELOADER

If the person is a Freeloader, you'll notice that there always seems to be an angle of getting something for free or at a reduced cost. Complaining that the meal is too salty or too bland in the hopes of not paying for it is just one example. Other common Freeloader moves are loading up on free items, sharing plates (but not wanting to pay the sharing charge), and trying to find ways to bring down the cost of everything.

The Freeloader is usually a hybrid between a Stiff and a Complainer: like Stiffs, they tend to be cheap on what they are paying for when it comes to menu items and drinks. And similar to the Complainer, they will nitpick about prices. However, Freeloaders have their own distinct characteristics that put them into a category all to themselves:

- Freeloading doesn't always relate to tipping. Yes, most Freeloaders exude a vibe of being cheap, but it's usually over the actual order. For example, a Freeloader may scheme to get a meal for free— even after eating 75 percent of it—but still leave a substantial tip.
- Freeloaders love the free parts of the meal, often taking an ungodly amount of bread or chips for example.
- The Freeloader may complain, but it's rarely about the service—it's about the price. Basically, this affects the restaurant more than the server, while a Stiff directly affects the server with his/her low/no tips.
- Freeloaders try to substitute the standard sides and combinations for more expensive ones, such as "Can I substitute a skewer of shrimp in place of the broccoli that comes with the entrée?"

Like other personality types, one quirky characteristic does not a Freeloader make, but instead Freeloaders exhibit a collection of conduct. And once you see a customer exhibiting a few of these traits you can be fairly confident you've spotted a Freeloader.

A common, yet egregious, example we recall is someone eating her entire plate and then complaining about it and wanting the charge taken off the bill. In another equally ridiculous instance, a waitress served a gentleman with very distinctive gray hair. He proceeded to eat the majority of his meal, and at the very end he showed her a gray hair on his plate. *That's* when he decided that the entrée should be removed from the bill! As a side note, there was absolutely no one working in that restaurant with visibly gray hair.

Of course, the server couldn't tell the man it was *his own* hair. Instead, he went to the manager and said, "There's a guy with gray hair who found a gray hair in his food, and now he wants it off the bill." The manager just laughed but then proceeded to take the meal off his bill. As wrong as it was, the manager handled it perfectly. You have to be 100 percent sure to call the Freeloader out on a move like that and would need a forensic crime lab to analyze the hair in question. It's just easier and more cost effective to take that item off the check and to be on the lookout for that Freeloader at a later date. More on that below.

Dealing with Freeloaders

Like it or not, the maxim "the customer is always right" is *the* law to live by when it comes to these situations. The H.E.A.T. acronym (see The Complainer) is especially effective here, too: hear the request or complaint, empathize, apologize about whatever has prompted the customer to ask for free items or price reductions, and then take action.

In this case, taking action will usually mean speaking to the manager. At that point, it is his or her call to make regarding the Freeloader's request. Most will probably honor the request, but at that point you can distance yourself from the issue.

Finally, the best thing you can do is try not to take it personally or get annoyed, even when it's clear the person is freeloading. Like a Stiff, this person is going to freeload even if you're not the server, and knowing this fact of life may help to ease your irritation as you go back to the kitchen to fetch the *tenth* helping of free chips and salsa!

THE CUSTOMIZER

If you remember the second-most infamous scenes from in "When Harry Met Sally," it's the scene where Sally is placing a food order: everything is "on the side," and she never orders anything off the menu as it is presented. Sally was a textbook Customizer.[3] Customizers vary in their degree of requests, ranging from the non-problematic Customizer who just doesn't want onions on his enchiladas to the more complex and abrasive Customizers who want to rewrite the meatloaf recipe. Obviously, it is dealing with the over-Customizer that requires a bit of finesse.

Here is a good example: A man ordered "The American Burger." It was a regular burger served on a Kaiser bun with lettuce, tomato, pickles, onions, and American cheese. This man chose to place that order and then asked us to omit the

---

3 If you have not yet watched "When Harry Met Sally" stop reading and watch it immediately. It's an American Classic with Meg Ryan when she was still Meg Ryan.

cheese, the bun, the pickles, the lettuce, *and* the onions! In its place, he requested mushroom gravy (which required the chef to make a roux and a gravy from scratch) and a smashed-out burger that would be a flatter steak shape. But that wasn't the end of it: he wanted no french fries, because he wanted to sub them out for mashed potatoes. That way, the mushroom gravy could be added to the potatoes as well! Essentially, the "American Burger" was being turned into a Salisbury steak. True story. If you have waited on tables for a week, you have likely already dealt with a Customizer and can relate to this scenario. Here is how you should handle it the next time you bump into one of these characters.

Dealing with Customizers

This personality type can be difficult for a server to handle, because you might not be aware if the chef can/will oblige the customer's request. When in doubt, the best thing to do is tell the customer to please wait for a moment while you check with the kitchen. You want to try to make the customer happy—that's the name of the game. That said, if you are in a restaurant that spells out on the menu that there are no substitutions—or they state what they can and can't substitute—it makes your job easier when you encounter a Customizer. You just point to the menu and say "I'm really sorry, I would love to do that for you, but for whatever reason, they won't allow me to." If your Customizer is insistent and says, for instance, "They always do this for me" or "This is how I did it last time." put down your pen and grab the manager and ask for a little guidance.

Looking at this from the chef's perspective may also help you handle crazy menu-modification requests. For many chefs, the menu is lovingly prepared. It's like their baby. If the chef does a parmesan herb risotto and it's his go-to item, it's his art. If you tell him to leave out any of the herbs or to use sharp cheddar instead of parmesan, you're messing with the chef's art. So understand if the chef gets miffed, it's not you—it's the Customizer's request that is an insult. Most chefs know, however, the only risotto that matters is the risotto that gets the customers back in the door. Setting pride aside and accommodating the customer whenever possible is always a safe and solid move.

Extreme customizing will most likely affect the prep time, so it may help to let the customer know that in a polite way. (By the way, in the case of the Salisbury steak customer, he complained that it took too long to make his dinner!)

Depending upon your experience, you might already know what the chef will and will not accept when Customizers make a request. In this case, you may be able to get away with telling the customer "yes" or "no" to certain requests on the spot, rather than checking with the chef first. In restaurants where we worked for a long time, we built up a certain comfort level with the other staff. We already knew what would or wouldn't upset the chef, so when we met up with a request that we knew would head south quickly, we would simply say, "We are sorry, but that can't be done." Then swiftly follow up with something that may be a good compromise: "However, let me suggest this . . ." or, "Why don't we . . ." or, "Maybe you'll like this instead . . ." In this way, you are attempting to customize within parameters that will please the customer and the chef. For instance, if the person is suggesting you take the sauce off the pizza, a calzone may be a perfectly acceptable substitute that you could suggest. In the restaurant business its important to avoid saying "no" as much as possible and instead give the customer appealing options if you are unable to satisfy their initial request.

THE MESS MAKER

This type of customer may be extremely friendly, funny, and kind, but pleasantries notwithstanding, Mess Makers can create tons of extra work for you during your shift. And even though some restaurants have bussers, it's still the server's job to keep his/her table clean during the meal. So when you have messy customers, the server is left to contend with what the Mess Maker leaves in their wake: sugar packets all over the table, bread crumbs everywhere, lemons lying around—you get the picture.

Please note that kids are an exception; we've seen little kids in high chairs throwing rice grenades everywhere, and that's understandable. In fact, we've walked up to tables with small children where we feel like we are surveying a tornado scene with chips, rice, and applesauce under the table, strewn around the table—all over the place. And even though babies themselves are adorable, sometimes the parents think the mess is cute, too, and will say things like, "That's our little baby! Look how she drops everything. Isn't that precious?"

While it would be nice to see these parents attempt to clean up after their tiny patrons, it's not their job, it's the server's job, and while we are sure you really appreciate it when parents tend to the disaster their kid created, a professional server would say something like, "We'll take care of it; that's what we're here for." Indeed, this is a solid strategy for turning the burden of cleaning the mess up into a blessing by earning bigger tips from those parents who are not ignorant of the additional work they are creating for the server.

Mess Makers, on the other hand, are a different story: they are fully-grown, they *should* know better, but they make no attempt to clean up after themselves. Here is a good example: One of us used to work at a country club where several trash cans lined the patio next to where customers sat. On one particularly busy day, there were four guys sitting right next to those trash cans, drinking beers and eating chips with salsa. After several hours, approximately thirty empty beer bottles were on the table—so many bottles that some of them were actually rolling around! It would have taken four seconds and minimal effort other than lifting an arm to toss a few of the bottles into the adjacent trash bins, but not one of them threw a single bottle away! Not a single one. Of course, the table should have been pre-bussed and those empties should have been cleared earlier by the server or staff, but you get the picture. Mess Makers seem to think that they are getting more value for their dollar by creating a bigger mess to be cleaned up once they leave. It's crazy. But it's true.

At the other end of the spectrum, there are Neat Eaters and Stackers, both of whom are a server's dream (well, a work-related dream anyway). Neat Eaters don't leave crumbs, and if they make a mess they are quick to clean it. Stackers take it one step further: they finish their plates, stack them, and then push them to the edge of the table for easy pick-up. Stackers are most likely servers or ex-servers; professional servers love waiting on other seasoned servers (who are usually Stackers and rarely Stiffs).

Unfortunately, Neat Eaters and Stackers are the minority with Mess Makers comprising a much larger portion of restaurant patron population. Regardless, Servers can handle these human trash tornadoes by taking a proactive 'maintenance' approach to the table.

Dealing with Mess Makers

As frustrating as they can be, just do your best to keep your server section clean when having to contend with a Mess Maker. Dealing with a Mess Maker effectively will require being at the table more frequently than your standard practice or than we would recommend for a normal table. There is no need to be obnoxious about your constant efforts to maintain the table; just be prompt and not overly dramatic. And certainly do not mention it or even bring up the fact that the table would be trashed if you weren't hovering over it. Obviously, you're not going to whip out the vacuum cleaner during the meal (because that *would* be rude), but you can stay on top of the quick and easy clean-ups. That way, without saying a word, you're communicating to the customer that you're trying to keep the table clean for them. Best of all, sometimes the Mess Maker may actually pick up on what's happening and become more attuned to the mess he or she is making. When that happens, it's a win-win for both of you, because they appreciate your attentive service and they are becoming a more thoughtful restaurant customer.

THE NOISE MAKERS

The Noise Makers are a table of multiple folks (not just a two-top) who are so entertained with each other that there are oblivious to what is going on around the table and are louder than is appropriate.

Obviously, acceptable rowdiness and noise levels varies depending upon the establishment and its atmosphere. If people are being loud and rowdy at a gastro pub or while watching a UFC fight on TV, the threshold for acceptable behaviour is expected to be lower and a higher noise level is appropriate.

Wine bars and steak houses, for example, are mellow, and in that type of atmosphere a loud and rowdy person is more obvious and obnoxious than they would be in a bar. To be sure, the Noise Makers impact other diners' experiences negatively. And many times, A Noisy Table will prompt other patrons to ask: "Can you get that guy/table to be quiet?" This a super awkward situation for a server. How do you ask someone to lower his or her voice without sounding rude yourself? Even though we've sometimes told the customer that we would tell the loud person to quiet down, we hardly ever follow through—not because we were ignoring the request but because we knew it wouldn't be well received.

Noise Makers are not only loud, sometimes they are just plain rude. See if any of these are familiar:

- You're trying to greet the table and share the specials of the day. As you educate the table about the menu and specials, someone at that table may continue talking and ignore you. Or people at the table continue their conversations and otherwise ignore your opening monologue so that you have to repeat the specials with each order you take.
- You greet the table, and the customer doesn't even say hello. You say, "How is everyone?" and the response is, "Bud Light." (Unfortunately, this one happens all the time.)
- You approach the table and the customer keeps talking on his or her phone. Obviously, it's a huge no-

no, but this is happening more and more frequently.[4]

4   We now live in a world where people work from their phones con-
    stantly, so while it's not acceptable to ask someone to put the phone
    away, it's definitely rude for the customer to refuse to unplug while
    the server is trying to wait on the table.

Dealing with Noise Makers

If the person/table is loud, one tactic is to speak more loudly yourself—without being too obvious. Simply approach the table with authority and project your voice. Don't be rude yourself, but definitely make yourself loud enough to be heard.

Another strategy is to look that person right in the eye while you're talking and explaining the specials. Get the loud or rude person's attention by making eye contact, and many times the person (or people) will actually pay attention.

Finally, a simple method that works well is killing the customer with kindness. There is definitely a fine line between being kind and being sarcastic, so you'll want to consider your delivery as you're speaking. But if you are kind and can get the person/people smiling, this will many times soften them and the Noisy Table will be a touch more respectful.

THE FLAGGER

Another name for this type of person is the "only-person-in-the-restaurant guy." This is the type of customer who, while you're greeting another table, will be shouting to you, raising a napkin, or even whistling to get your attention because they would like more wine, napkins, butter for their bread, etc. The Flagger can't wait for you to be free to address his concerns, because he is hopelessly clueless to the fact that there are other people who deserve your time and attention too.

Flaggers truly feel like they're the only ones that you have to serve. To be fair, they may not know any better. Flaggers are the kind of people who think servers are the same as butlers. That said, here are a few strategies for dealing with the Flagger.

Dealing with Flaggers

Try letting the person know that you have seen their flagging and will address their request as soon as you can. Even if you can't immediately get to the Flagger because you're in the middle of another task, you can smile or nod to let them know that you have seen them and acknowledge that he/she needs something—and then get over to there as quickly as possible once you have completed what you need to complete.

In addition, you can educate the Flagger in a polite way. For example, when you approach the table after being flagged, you can say something like, "Hey, I totally understand; let me get that for you. I apologize, but I was taking care of another table. Actually, I have five other tables that I am taking care of right now, but let me get that for you right away." This lets the Flagger know he or she isn't the only customer, and sometimes this alone will create a level of awareness within that person. At the very least, you're empathizing with your customer but kindly asserting yourself to explain that you're not being slow or inattentive but that you also have other responsibilities. You can even subtly share those priorities: "Let me get the other table their hot food first, and then I will be right back with your butter." Many patrons understand that hot items take precedence and might not be so impatient with getting what they need.

Exercise: Track Your Customers

We are not talking about stalking customers, but now that we have identified some of the most common types of annoying customer behaviors, keep tabs on the customers you're interacting with. Over the next week, note how many of the customer types you see and/or serve and reflect on how you would have responded to each. Is there one type that annoys you more than others? Which types do you deal with the best? Which types are you least effective with? For customers who really bother you, experiment with the suggestions in this chapter and notice how your stress level and customer interactions begin to improve.

While the world will always have annoying and rude customers for you to serve, you can start taking the steps we have set out for you today to deal with them and keep your sanity while doing it!

AFTERWORD

As you may recall, in step 4, we encourage you to tip-out cheerfully. But we encourage you not to stop there. At the end of each shift, tip-out for the greater good by setting aside ten percent of what you earn to donate to charity. Servers of faith will not be shocked by this concept, as they are likely familiar with charitable giving as part of their own spiritual program. It is certainly Biblical, for in the Bible it is written: "For God loves a cheerful giver" (2 Corinthians 9:7) and "Bring the whole tithe into the storehouse, that there may be food in my house. Test me in this," says the Lord Almighty, "and see if I will not throw open the floodgates of heaven and pour out so much blessing that you will not have room enough for it." (Malachi 3:10).

For Muslims, that act of charity known as Zakaah, is a part of the "Five Pillars of Islam" and is mandatory. Tithing is also encouraged in the Buddhist, Hindu, and Sikh faiths. The practice of setting aside money for charity has clearly been around long before restaurants. In *See You at the Top*, Zig Ziglar perfectly described the benefits of giving, in our opinion:

This I guarantee. If you will do something for someone who is unable to return the favor, you will get a lot more than you could possibly give. In so many cases, what you give will mean much to the recipient, but the feeling you get when you do something for someone who cannot do for themselves is indescribable. You will realize that you are truly fortunate, that you do have a lot to be thankful for, that you can make a contribution and that you are in fact somebody. In short, you will stand tall in your own eyes, which is the bonus you get because you took what you had and unselfishly used it for someone else's good.

Charles Dickens said it best: "No one is useless in this world who lightens the burden of it to anyone else."

But even secular, or at least not openly religious sources, encourage the practice of charitable giving as part of blueprint for successful living. For example, in his *Awaken the Giant Within*, the world-renowned personal achievement coach, Anthony Robbins, asserts "Living is giving." And the giving should be done cheerfully. He advises:

> Don't fall into the trap, though, of trying to contribute to others at your own expense— playing the martyr won't give you a true sense of contribution. But if you can consistently give to yourself and others on a measurable scale that allows you to know that your life has mattered, you'll have a sense of connection with people and a sense of pride and self-esteem that no amount of money, accomplishments, fame or acknowledgment could ever give.

Thus, if you are a server of faith, you will reap what you sow when you tip-out to charity. If you are not of this mind-set, you will nevertheless feel great about yourself while you make a meaningful difference in the world with your charitable giving. We strongly encourage you to tip-out cheerfully. It will make an enormously positive difference in your life. If you have any doubts about this, we encourage you to try an experiment. Tip-out cheerfully and give 5% of your cash tips to a charity for a week. Then see how you feel.

Remember, the first 10 percent of everything we earn from this project will go to help feeding hungry people—a good and laudable goal indeed. Your charitable giving could also make a huge impact on this or any other endeavor you chose to pursue to benefit the greater good. Living is giving. And the more we give the more we get. It's pretty simple really. So get giving!

ABOUT THE AUTHORS

Each of us firmly believes that we would not be who we are today but for our experience of serving other people in a restaurant. These experiences have shaped who we are as service providers in our respective post-table-waiting professions. Our combined experience has left us with this undeniable truth—the better we treat others the better our own lives become.

James Caldwell

Jim is the President and General Counsel of a marine service and construction company in Houston, TX. When he is not working, Jim is either with his wife and three daughters or some assortment thereof, exercising, reading, laughing or watching stuff on television about World War II. He is also active in his church and firmly believes that a person is what he thinks he is. At least he thinks so.

Patrick Caldwell

Patrick is a writer and patent attorney living in Nagoya, Japan. When not working or studying Japanese, he is busy trying to eat in every single ramen shop in Aichi prefecture. Sometimes his wife drags him out to nonfood-related travel throughout Asia.

Michael Rathke

Michael is a full-time photographer. He is happily married and just welcomed his first child, a baby girl. When he is not taking portraits, Michael is sleeping or eating. He also enjoys his role as "the funny one" in the family. Just ask Jim Caldwell (his brother in-law).

Brady Smith

Brady lives in LA with his wife, daughter and baby boy. He makes his living as an actor (go ahead "Google" him) and does art when he has the time. He also raises chickens, dives with sharks, and surfs, but not in that order.

BONUS FOR READERS OF THIS BOOK

Get a free copy of our "Rules for Restaurant Customers" which are 10 guidelines for the way we hope all customers could behave in restaurants.

Download your copy here:
(www.GetBiggerTips.com)